WHO NEEDS
CHRISTMAS

ANDY STANLEY

NORTH POINT
RESOURCES

ZONDERVAN™

ZONDERVAN
Who Needs Christmas Study Guide
Copyright © 2019 by North Point Ministries, Inc.

Requests for information should be addressed to:
Zondervan, *3900 Sparks Dr. SE, Grand Rapids, Michigan 49546*

ISBN 978-0-310-12107-7 (softcover)
ISBN 978-0-310-12108-4 (ebook)

First Printing September 2019 / Printed in the United States of America

[CONTENTS]

Using the Study Guide 5

Introduction 7

Session One: *The Story Behind the Story* 11

Session Two: *The Author of Life* 21

Session Three: *The Message of Christmas* 33

Session Four: *Ready or Not . . . He Is Coming* 43

Leader's Guide 55

USING THE
STUDY GUIDE

BEFORE THE FIRST GROUP MEETING

Read through the Introduction for an overview of the study.

Flip through pages 11–20 to understand the layout of a session.

DURING EACH GROUP MEETING

1. Turn to the Video Notes page and watch the video segment.

2. Use the Discussion Questions to have a conversation about the video content.

AFTER EACH GROUP MEETING

On your own, read the Think About It section.

Review the Before the Next Session section at the end of each session and complete the tasks.

[INTRODUCTION]

The Christmas season is upon us again. And that can be challenging for many reasons.

For most of us, life gets busy during the holidays. There just aren't enough hours to work, take care of our homes, go to our kids' school programs, shop, decorate, and get all of those cards signed, stamped, and sent to our families and friends.

Christmas can also bring the stress of managing difficult family relationships through tense meals and uncomfortable conversations. And it can be a painful reminder of loved ones who are no longer with us.

Whether you think Christmas is the most wonderful time of the year or a month of busyness you hope to put behind you with as little fuss as possible, we hope this study helps you press pause, take a deep breath (or dozens of deep breaths), and connect with your heavenly Father—*really* connect with him.

That, after all, is what Christmas is truly about. It's our opportunity to remember an event that changed the world. It's a reminder that no matter what life throws at us, God loves us. He loves us so much that he chose to send his one and only Son into this world as a helpless infant, **who would make the ultimate sacrifice for us.**

In a way, the most challenging thing about Christmas isn't the hectic pace, the shopping, the decorating, or even the abrasive, opinionated family members. The most challenging thing about Christmas is the Christmas story. The story of Jesus' birth is so miraculous and amazing that it's hard to believe. It sounds too good to be true.

It's tempting to think, *Jesus' followers came up with this myth about him being born to a virgin in order to give him street cred later on. It didn't really happen. It couldn't have really happened. Virgins don't get pregnant and give birth.* But consider this: During his earthly ministry, Jesus predicted his death and resurrection . . . and then he pulled it off. If he could do that, maybe we shouldn't be all that concerned about the improbability of the circumstances of his birth.

Maybe we should consider that God did something improbable on purpose because he wanted us to know that he was moving in the world in order to change the world—forever.

That's what we'll explore over the next four sessions. And we hope that exploration changes your perspective on the Christmas season.

[THE STORY BEHIND THE STORY]

The story of Christmas doesn't begin the way you probably think it does. It doesn't begin with angels announcing the birth of a savior. It doesn't begin with a young couple on an out-of-town trip trying to find a place to stay as the woman goes into labor. It begins all the way back in the beginning, in the book of Genesis.

OVERVIEW

Two thousand years before Jesus was born, God made a promise to a man named Abram, who we would eventually know as Abraham. It wasn't just any promise. It was an unbelievable, incoherent, impossible promise. And yet it set up the events around Christmas.

> The LORD had said to Abram, "Go from your country, your people and your father's household to the land I will show you.
>
> "I will make you into a great nation,
> and I will bless you;

I will make your name great,

and you will be a blessing.

I will bless those who bless you,

and whoever curses you I will curse;

and all peoples on earth

will be blessed through you." Genesis 12:1–3

At this point, Abram was about 75 years old with no children. It's an understatement to say that it looked impossible that his descendants would ever become a nation, let alone that they would bless all the people on earth. But the author of Genesis tells us that *Abraham believed the unbelievable*. He made a choice that, no matter how improbable God's promises seemed given his current circumstances, he could trust them.

Then what happened? Abraham eventually had a son named Isaac. Isaac had a son named Jacob, and Jacob had twelve sons. One of them, Joseph, was sold into slavery in Egypt by 10 of his brothers. But he rose to a position of influence with the Pharaoh and saved his family and the Egyptians from famine. Within a few generations, Abraham's offspring had grown into a nation—but they were a nation of slaves inside Egypt. They didn't feel blessed. And they certainly didn't seem to be in a position to bless all the people on earth.

Hundreds of years later, God sent Moses to deliver his people from slavery. By the time Moses was done, no one in Egypt was feeling blessed by Abraham's descendants. God led his people into the Promised Land, but that created conflict with those already living there. Again, few people were feeling blessed by Abraham's descendants.

It can be challenging for us to read about all of the violence and war in the Old Testament. That doesn't seem like something a loving God would allow. But it was commonplace in the ancient world, and it has been commonplace throughout most of human history.

We only find it offensive because we live on the other side of Christmas. We see the world in a completely different way, but this was part of the journey. And that journey produced the kingdom of Israel, ruled most famously by David and his son Solomon. It was a kingdom that had the power and wealth to bless people across the earth . . . but it didn't.

Instead, Israel was split in two. Eventually, the Assyrians overran the Southern Kingdom, and the Babylonians took the Northern Kingdom into exile. Hundreds of years went by and the fulfillment of God's promises to Abraham seemed more impossible than ever.

There was no reason for the people of Israel to believe God's promises. But here's what God said to the nation during this difficult time through the prophet Malachi:

> "My name will be great among the nations, from where
> the sun rises to where it sets." Malachi 1:11

To the people of Israel, this must have seemed ridiculous. God's name was being mocked among the nations. His name was a joke. No one from the surrounding nations was looking at the fate of Israel and thinking, *I want to worship their God*. Israel couldn't feed or protect itself. It looked like a nation on its last legs.

Then, in 63 BC, Rome sent Pompey the Great to the area of Judah in Galilee. He conquered town after town until he was outside the walls of Jerusalem, the capital of Israel. And so began the Roman occupation of what came to be called the Holy Land. For 400 years, God's promises to Abraham seemed to be null and void.

But then an extraordinary thing happened. Looking back on it years later, trying to put the whole story together, the apostle Paul wrote:

> "But when the set time had fully come, God sent his Son,
> born of a woman, born under the law . . ." Galatians 4:4

When nobody was expecting it, God sent the angel Gabriel to Nazareth, a town in Galilee, to a virgin pledged to be married to a man named Joseph, a descendant of King David.

The virgin's name was Mary. The angel went to her and said, "Greetings, you who are highly favored! The Lord is with you."

Mary was greatly troubled at his words and wondered what kind of greeting this might be. But the angel said to her, "Do not be afraid, Mary; you have found favor with God. You will conceive and give birth to a son, and you are to call him Jesus. He will be great and will be called the Son of the Most High. The Lord God will give him the throne of his father David, and he will reign over Jacob's descendants forever; his kingdom will never end." Luke 1:27–33

It turns out the Jewish people *would* be a blessing to the people of earth. And the thing that makes the Christmas story so believable is the fact that the story—the whole story—is so remarkable. No one would have made it up. No one *could* have made it up. It stretched over so many years that the thread wasn't always evident. People lost track. People lost sight.

But God was working behind the scenes, setting the stage. The Christmas story began 2,000 years before the first Christmas. And it continues to unfold 2,000 years later.

So, who needs Christmas? God decided the world needed Christmas.

VIDEO NOTES

_____
_____
_____
_____
_____
_____
_____
_____
_____
_____
_____
_____
_____
_____
_____
_____
_____

DISCUSSION QUESTIONS

1. How do you feel heading into this Christmas season? Is it a positive or negative time for you?

2. Do you find it difficult to believe the details of the Christmas story? Why or why not?

3. Talk about a time when God seemed silent or distant in your life. What happened? What did that experience do for your faith?

4. Read Genesis 12:1-3. In what ways does God's promise to Abraham change your view of the Christmas story?

5. Read Isaiah 49:6. What does this verse tell you about God's character?

6. What can you do this season to focus on the meaning of the Christmas story in our culture and in your life? How can this group help you?

THINK ABOUT IT

Christmas reminds us in the most remarkable way that God is active even when he feels distant or absent. Even when God is silent, he is not still. Through this remarkable story, we are reminded on a personal level that God cares about us. He doesn't just think in terms of nations; he knows us as individuals.

God didn't just send his Son to be the Savior of the world. He sent Jesus to be your Savior in your world.

The Christmas story means that despite challenging circumstances, we can trust God. Even when it seems like God can't possibly care about us, he is present, he is listening, and he keeps his promises.

Why Christmas?

Because the world needed Christmas.

The world needed hope.

The world needed the Light of the World.

BEFORE THE NEXT SESSION

To prepare for your next session, read the Overview for Session Two. Feel free to also look through the Discussion Questions.

During the week, spend some time each day reading the following passages in your Bible: Matthew 1:18–25, Romans 5:1–11.

[THE AUTHOR OF LIFE]

The apostle Paul was at first a rich, powerful Christian hater. When he became a Jesus follower, he began to see the Jewish scriptures in a new way. He realized the Old Testament was the story of how God brought something brand-new into the world.

Paul wrote:

> "But when the set time had fully come, God sent his Son . . ." Galatians 4:4

In other words, when God had things exactly the way he wanted them, when he had the world's undivided attention, when he knew human history had gotten to a place where the story would not be forgotten, he did something extraordinary.

OVERVIEW

When the set time had fully come, God sent his Son. But here's the question we'll wrestle with this session, because it's the Christmas question: *Why?* Why did God have to send his Son? Why couldn't he just send a messenger?

It gets even more complicated. The apostle Paul wrote:

> "But when the set time had fully come, God sent his Son, born of a woman, born under the law . . ." Galatians 4:4

Why did God have to come as a baby? Why did he have to be like the rest of us—not a law unto himself, but born *under the law* and accountable to it?

It was because God wanted to do what laws and regulations could not. He wanted to do what judges and prophets could not. He wanted to do what exile and punishment could not. He wanted to do what even sacred texts could not.

God wanted to do something *personal*, so he had to do something *relational*.

God wanted to do something for you personally. He wanted to do something for each one of us personally. He didn't want to simply move nations or tribes. He wanted to move individuals into a personal relationship with himself. So, at Christmas, God took the first step toward removing every obstacle to unrestricted fellowship with him. He began to break down all of the barriers between you and him.

This was personal, so he had to come. He entered into history in such a way that people would know about it thousands of years later. They would remember it. Don't miss the gravity of the history of the story of Christmas. Four thousand years ago, God promised he would do something through the line of Abraham. Two thousand years later, Jesus was born. And two thousand years after that, we're still talking about it.

Think about how many significant things have happened over the past 2,000 years. Most weren't written down. History has forgotten them. Yet the birth of a Jewish baby in the armpit of the Roman Empire is celebrated all over the world every year because God carefully orchestrated the event so we wouldn't miss it. He made sure we would remember.

In his letter to the first-century church in Rome, the apostle Paul explains it this way:

> But God demonstrates his own love for us in this: While we were still sinners, Christ died for us. Romans 5:8

Notice Paul used the present tense. He wrote, "While we were still sinners, Christ died for us." That's hard for us to comprehend because God sent his Son long before we were born. He demonstrated his love for us before we even existed. But Jesus died for Paul while he was still sinning. He was still resisting God. And Jesus' sacrifice was just as much for each of us as it was for Paul. We have all resisted God.

So, the question that follows "Why did God have to send his Son?" is: "Why did Jesus have to die?" If God makes the rules, why couldn't he just declare everyone forgiven? Why did death have to factor into the equation?

It was because God is the author of life. Life is sophisticated. It's complicated. In some ways, your cells are smarter than your brain. Your body is doing things you aren't even aware of. And when you dishonor the source of life, you dishonor life itself. In other words, we owe God our lives, and our disregard for God forfeited our right to life.

We owe a debt to the Giver of Life that we can't pay. But God demonstrates his love for us in that while we were still sinners, Christ died in our place. Christ died *for us.*

After Jesus rose from the dead, his disciples went out into the streets of Jerusalem and began to speak to the very people who had Jesus arrested and crucified. Peter said:

> "You killed the author of life, but God raised him from the dead. We are witnesses of this." Acts 3:15

The author of life gave away his life. You cannot take the life of the author of life unless he allows it. God sent his Son into this world as a baby to grow up *like* us and *among* us so he could give what we owed and could not give.

Jesus' death demonstrated the magnitude of our ingratitude and the severity of our offense. But it also demonstrated the magnitude of God's love for us.

Why did Jesus have to die? Because you cannot demonstrate love without sacrifice. Words are cheap. Love must be shown to be known. And the only way to show love is to give up something for the one you love. You'll never know how much someone really cares for you until you see what they're willing to sacrifice for you. The fact that God gave up his one and only Son demonstrates the incredible depth of his love for us.

So, when the set time had fully come, when everyone had given up hope, a Jewish carpenter discovered his fiancée was pregnant. As he was trying to figure out what to do with that information, the angel of the Lord spoke to him:

> "Joseph son of David, do not be afraid to take Mary home as your wife, because what is conceived in her is from the Holy Spirit. She will give birth to a son, and you are to give him the name Jesus, because he will save his people from their sins." Matthew 1:20–21

All of this took place to fulfill what the Lord had said through the prophet Isaiah:

> The virgin will conceive and give birth to a son, and will call him Immanuel. Isaiah 7:14

Do you know what the name "Immanuel" means? It means "God with us." God staged a demonstration and documented it so the world would know. He made sure that 2,000 years later, *we* would know it.

We needed to know that the story of Christmas was about us.

VIDEO NOTES

DISCUSSION QUESTIONS

1. Talk about a time you had trouble convincing someone else of something you knew to be true. What happened?

2. Read Galatians 4:4–7. In what ways does our culture tempt us to behave like slaves even though we're God's children?

3. In the video teaching, Andy said, "The events of Christmas would be unbelievable if the story wasn't so remarkable." Do you find the Christmas story unbelievable or remarkable? What are some of the things that have shaped your view of Christmas?

4. Read Romans 5:6–8. What are some truths about God that you wouldn't know if Jesus hadn't demonstrated them?

5. In the video teaching, Andy said, "Jesus' death demonstrated the magnitude of our ingratitude and the magnitude of his love for us." Is it difficult for you to believe God loves you that much? Why or why not?

6. What can you do this Christmas season to show gratitude for God's choice to demonstrate his love for you? How can this group help you?

7. If happiness is powered by the law of the harvest, what do you need to "sow" in your life right now so that you can "reap" happiness in the future? How can this group support you?

THINK ABOUT IT

Jesus' disciple John said it best:

> For God so loved the world that he gave his one and
> only Son, that whoever believes in him shall not perish
> but have eternal life. John 3:16

The phrase "believe in" means "trust." It's not just believing that Jesus existed. Nor is it like believing in Santa Claus. There's nothing magical about it. Trusting in Jesus means relying on him as the source of your relationship with your heavenly Father. It means trusting that God loves *you* so much that he orchestrated the Christmas story in human history so that despite your sin, you could reconnect with the author of life.

That's why God had to send his Son. It's why he couldn't just send a messenger.

BEFORE THE NEXT SESSION

To prepare for your next session, read the Overview for Session Three. Feel free to also look through the Discussion Questions.

During the week, spend some time reading Romans 6:1–14.

SESSION THREE
[THE MESSAGE OF CHRISTMAS]

Fun fact: The name Jesus is a Latin translation of the Greek word for the Jewish name *Yeshua*. That's where we get the name Joshua in English. It may mess up your Christmas music to know that we've been mispronouncing Jesus' name.

It's okay. You don't have to start calling Jesus "Joshua." But it's important to understand there's a connection between Jesus and the Joshua of the Old Testament—the Joshua who was Moses' protégé and who led God's people into the Promised Land. More important, the Old Testament prophets made a connection between Joshua and the Messiah God had promised his people.

The Old Testament Joshua was a warrior. He was a general. And that's what first-century Jews expected of the Messiah. Remember, they were a subject nation. Their country was occupied by the Roman Empire. They hoped and dreamed of a Joshua-like Messiah who would rise up and drive Rome's fierce military out of the land.

Jesus—*Yeshua*—challenged all of their assumptions.

OVERVIEW

How did the birth of the Messiah come about? That's what we're going to talk about in this session.

Matthew's Gospel tells us that Jesus' mother, Mary, was pledged to be married to Joseph, but before they came together, she was found to be pregnant by the Holy Spirit. When Joseph discovered this, he chose to quietly end their engagement. Why did he keep it quiet? He may have just wanted to minimize the harm to her and the shame to her family. But let's be honest: He may have thought she was crazy. *She believed she was pregnant by the Holy Spirit?* Joseph may have decided it would be cruel to take vengeance on someone with mental health issues.

But then something extraordinary happened:

> . . . an angel of the Lord appeared to him in a dream and said, "Joseph son of David, do not be afraid to take Mary home as your wife, because what is conceived in her is from the Holy Spirit. She will give birth to a son, and you are to give him the name Jesus, because he will save his people from their sins."

All this took place to fulfill what the Lord had said through the prophet: "The virgin will conceive and give birth to a son, and they will call him Immanuel" (which means "God with us"). Matthew 1:20–23

Now here's what you need to know—especially if you find the idea of the virgin birth difficult to believe. The Hebrew word for "virgin" in the prophecy quoted by the angel (Isaiah 7:14) can also mean "maiden" or "young girl." So, no one in the first century expected the Messiah to be born of a virgin. For Matthew to have manufactured that detail doesn't help the storyline. The only reason this detail made it into the narrative is because it's true. No one rallied around the virgin birth. Early Christians rallied around the resurrection.

Yet Matthew tells us that an angel appeared to Mary and to Joseph in dreams and told them their son was special. The Holy Spirit of God had conceived him. And the angel told them to name this son Jesus—*Yeshua*, Joshua. Joseph understood that the angel commanded him to give his son the name of the long-awaited warrior-king.

And the angel told Joseph, "He will save his people." Joseph hoped, like everyone hoped, that the Messiah would save his people from the oppression of the Romans. But the angel said something very different: "He will save his people *from their sins.*"

That's not what Joseph expected. It's not the image of the Messiah that people had built in their imaginations. They weren't looking for someone to save them from their sins. They didn't think they needed to be saved from their sins. They believed they had a religious system—the law—that allowed them to make restitution for sin. What Joseph and his people wanted was to be saved from the Romans.

If we're honest with ourselves, we're not much different. The idea of being saved from our sins doesn't move us—even those of us who follow Jesus. Most of us don't fall to our knees, feel emotional, or sense something powerful when we hear that God sent Jesus to save us from our sins. That's because we don't usually think of Jesus as saving us from our sins. We think of him as *forgiving us for our sins.* It's a subtle but important difference.

If we're not careful, we can reduce Christmas to forgiveness. We think, *Nobody's perfect, but God forgives.* For many people, that's their entire religious experience. But the message of Christmas is bigger than that. And if you've reduced Christmas to forgiveness, you've missed the message of Christmas.

Jesus didn't come to deliver us from the *consequences* of sin. In fact, most of the time we still have to face the consequences of our sins. Jesus came to deliver us from the *power* of sin. Jesus came in the spirit of Joshua, the warrior, to free us from slavery to sin. Over and over in the Gospels, Jesus tells people to leave their lives of sin. But is that even possible? Can we actually say no to sin?

In John's Gospel, Jesus was talking to the Pharisees when he said:

> "The thief comes only to steal and kill and destroy; I have come that they may have life, and have it to the full." John 10:10

That sounds bigger than forgiveness, doesn't it? Forgiveness evens the score. "Life to the full" is a kind of freedom most of us don't experience. In his letter to the Romans, the apostle Paul described it this way:

> Therefore do not let sin reign in your mortal body so that you obey its evil desires. Do not offer any part of yourself to sin as an instrument of wickedness, but rather offer yourselves to God as those who have been brought from death to life; and offer every part of

yourself to him as an instrument of righteousness. For sin shall no longer be your master, because you are not under the law, but under grace. Romans 6:12–14

Paul would say it is possible to be free from sin. We can say no to temptation. But only because of Jesus. That's why we need the message of Christmas.

VIDEO NOTES

DISCUSSION QUESTIONS

1. What is one of your favorite Christmas memories? Why is it special to you?

2. Read John 10:10. Is it difficult to believe that Jesus wants you to have life to the full? Why or why not?

3. Do you tend to view the story of Christmas as Jesus providing forgiveness for your sins or as Jesus setting you free from sin? What has shaped your view of the Christmas story?

4. Is it difficult for you to believe that sin doesn't have to be your master and that Jesus has set you free? Why or why not?

5. Read Romans 6:12-14. What do you think it would look like for you to "offer yourself to God"? How would your daily life be different?

6. Does sin currently master you? What can you do to remind yourself that sin is not your master because Jesus has set you free? How can this group support you?

THINK ABOUT IT

Becoming a follower of Jesus is as simple as saying, "God, I believe Jesus is your Son, sent into this world to die for my sins. I'm placing all of my trust in the fact that his death on the cross paid for all of my sin."

In that moment, according to Scripture and according to what Jesus taught, you become a child of God. You are adopted into his family because you freely receive what he freely offers.

If you've never accepted this offer, or if you made the choice as a small child but have wondered and had questions your entire adult life, consider praying that prayer.

The prayer doesn't make you a Christian; it's not a magic spell. The prayer is just a way to express that you're transferring your trust from your own goodness to what God, through Jesus, has done for you.

BEFORE THE NEXT SESSION

To prepare for your next session, read the Overview for Session Four. Feel free to also look through the Discussion Questions.

During the week, spend some time each day reading Luke 1 and 2 in your Bible.

SESSION FOUR

[READY OR NOT . . . HE IS COMING]

The first Christmas was the culmination of God's amazing plan that began 2,000 years before the birth of Christ. God spoke to an old man named Abram, who would later become Abraham. God told him that despite the fact he was old and had no children, his descendants would one day become a nation. God promised that Abraham would be famous (he is!) and that all earth's people would be blessed through him.

This probably didn't make sense to Abraham because there weren't really nations at that time—there were tribes. And tribes didn't bless other tribes. They stole from and warred against one another.

Abraham didn't always cooperate with the plan. He lied. He was selfish. He was often impatient. He sometimes treated people poorly. But it's as if God decided to bless the people of earth through Abraham *despite* Abraham.

God used imperfect, unbelieving, misbehaving people all along the way as he moved history toward the birth of Christ. In fact, every single person God used had a shaky, imperfect faith.

God used imperfect people to orchestrate the perfect story—the Christmas story.

OVERVIEW

The most famous version of the Christmas story appears in Luke's Gospel. Luke was a first-century Greek Gentile physician who sometimes traveled with the apostle Paul as Paul planted churches around the Mediterranean Rim. Luke wasn't an eyewitness to Jesus' earthly ministry; he became a Christ-follower later. But he interviewed Jesus' friends, family, and followers in order to write "an orderly account" of Jesus' life.

That account doesn't begin with the birth of Jesus. It doesn't begin with Mary and Joseph. It begins with a Jewish priest named Zechariah. He was one of about 20,000 priests that lived in and around Jerusalem. These priests were divided into groups and assigned the tasks that kept the temple running.

Against all odds, Zechariah was chosen to do the most unique job a priest could do. He was chosen to go into the Holy of Holies—the inner sanctuary of the tabernacle where God's presence dwelled in some sense. Every day, the priests would sacrifice to God in the morning, afternoon, or early evening, outside at the altar. They would pray for the nation of Israel. But before the morning sacrifice and after the afternoon or early evening sacrifice, a priest would go behind the thick curtain that separated the Holy of Holies from the rest of the tabernacle. Once inside, the priest would light incense.

There were so many priests that it was unlikely any particular one would ever be selected to go into the Holy of Holies. If you were selected, this would be the best day of your professional life.

When Zechariah went into the Holy of Holies, other priests were gathered outside in the inner room and out in the courtyard waiting for the incense to be lit. It was a dangerous job. Not just anybody could be in God's presence. In fact, it was custom to tie a rope around the ankle of a priest entering the Holy of Holies. If they died in God's presence, the other priests could drag them out without entering.

While Zechariah was inside, something amazing happened:

> Then an angel of the Lord appeared to him, standing at
> the right side of the altar of incense. When Zechariah
> saw him, he was startled and was gripped with fear. But
> the angel said to him: "Do not be afraid, Zechariah;
> your prayer has been heard. Your wife Elizabeth will
> bear you a son, and you are to call him John. He will be
> a joy and delight to you, and many will rejoice because
> of his birth, for he will be great in the sight of the Lord."
> Luke 1:11–15

Zechariah and his wife were old, and they had never been able to
have children. So he doubted. Despite the fact that he was in the
Holy of Holies and face to face with an angel, it seemed impossible
that his wife would have a baby. Here's what happened next:

> The angel said to him, "I am Gabriel. I stand in the
> presence of God, and I have been sent to speak to you
> and to tell you this good news. And now you will be
> silent and not able to speak until the day this happens,
> because you did not believe my words, which will come
> true at their appointed time." Luke 1:19–20

Zechariah lost the power to talk. He didn't say another word until Elizabeth had given birth:

> On the eighth day they came to circumcise the child, and they were going to name him after his father Zechariah, but his mother spoke up and said, "No! He is to be called John."
>
> They said to her, "There is no one among your relatives who has that name."
>
> Then they made signs to his father, to find out what he would like to name the child. He asked for a writing tablet, and to everyone's astonishment he wrote, "His name is John." Immediately his mouth was opened and his tongue set free, and he began to speak, praising God. All the neighbors were filled with awe, and throughout the hill country of Judea people were talking about all these things. Everyone who heard this wondered about it, asking, "What then is this child going to be?" For the Lord's hand was with him. Luke 1:59–66

And the Lord's hand was with John. As an adult, he was known as John the Baptist, chosen by God to prepare the people for the arrival of the Messiah. This brings us to the second pregnancy story Luke tells us in his Gospel . . .

In the sixth month of Elizabeth's pregnancy, God sent an angel to Nazareth, a town in Galilee, to a virgin pledged to be married to a man named Joseph, a descendant of David. You probably know the virgin's name. Most people do. It was Mary. That's significant because Luke records her response to the news that despite her virginity, she would be pregnant with the Messiah:

> "My soul glorifies the Lord
>> and my spirit rejoices in God my Savior,
>> for he has been mindful
>> of the humble state of his servant.
> From now on all generations will call me blessed,
>> for the Mighty One has done great things for me—
>> holy is his name. Luke 1:46–49

That may sound grandiose. It may even sound arrogant. But she was right, wasn't she? Two thousand years later, we know her name. We consider her blessed by God. The angel told her:

. . . "The Holy Spirit will come on you, and the power of the Most High will overshadow you. So the holy one to be born will be called the Son of God." Luke 1:35

Mary gave the perfect response. It wasn't based on her ability to understand God's plan. It was based on her confidence in the source of the information. She said, "May your word to me be fulfilled." Then the angel left her.

At Christmas—every Christmas—we're reminded that God is going to fulfill his word. He's going to do it despite our weaknesses, doubts, and second-guessing. Why? Because he loves us.

He loves us when we don't behave. He'll love us until we do behave. He'll love us if we never behave. He'll love us when we don't believe. He'll love us until we do believe. Your heavenly Father will love you if you never believe.

That's why we need the Christmas story.

VIDEO NOTES

DISCUSSION QUESTIONS

1. What are you looking forward to this Christmas season? Why?

2. Why is it important that people like Abraham and Zechariah were imperfect and sometimes weak in their faith, but God chose to include them in his plan to reconcile people to him?

3. Think about the story you heard of Zechariah entering the Holy of Holies with a rope tied around his foot in case the other priests had to drag him out. What does that indicate about how Jesus fundamentally changed our relationship with God?

4. Do you ever feel like you're not good enough or faithful enough for God to use your gifts and talents in his plans? If so, did this video change your perspective?

5. What can you do this Christmas to remind yourself that God is going to fulfill his word despite your weaknesses, doubts, and second-guessing?

6. God loves you so much that he sent his only Son to die in order to set you free from sin. How does that change your perspective on faith? How does it change your perspective on life?

THINK ABOUT IT

And there were shepherds living out in the fields nearby, keeping watch over their flocks at night. An angel of the Lord appeared to them, and the glory of the Lord shone around them, and they were terrified. But the angel said to them, "Do not be afraid. I bring you good news that will cause great joy for all the people. Today in the town of David a Savior has been born to you; he is the Messiah, the Lord. This will be a sign to you: You will find a baby wrapped in cloths and lying in a manger."

> Suddenly a great company of the heavenly host appeared with the angel, praising God and saying,
>
> "Glory to God in the highest heaven,
> and on earth peace to those on whom his favor rests."
>
> Luke 2:8–14

This Christmas, peace to you on whom God's favor rests—not because of you, and perhaps in spite of you. Ready or not, believe it or not, God sent his Son into the world to save us from our sins . . . because he loves us.

BEFORE CHRISTMAS

We hope you enjoyed this study and connected more with your group. During the time you have between the end of this study and Christmas Day, try to slow down your pace. Use this time to connect in meaningful ways with your heavenly Father.

We recommend you spend some time reading Luke 1 and 2. Consider reading each chapter a few times over the course of a week. When you read a chapter, pause to think about what details stood out to you (maybe for the first time).

Spend some time praying as well. Most of us spend a lot of our prayer time asking God for things we need or want. Instead, focus on thanking him for providing what you *really* need: a Savior.

[LEADER'S GUIDE]

LEADING THE DISCUSSION

You probably have a mental picture of what it will look like to lead—what you'll say and how group members will respond. Before you get too far into planning, there are some things you should know about leading a small-group discussion.

CULTIVATE DISCUSSION

It's easy to assume that a group meeting lives or dies on the quality of your ideas. That's not true. It's the ideas of everyone in the group that make a meeting successful. Your role is to create an environment in which people feel safe to share their thoughts. That's how relationships will grow and thrive among your group members.

Here's a basic truth about spiritual growth within the context of community: the study materials aren't as important as the relationships through which those materials take practical shape in the lives of the group members. The more meaningful the relationships, the more meaningful the study. The best materials in the world won't change lives in a sterile environment.

POINT TO THE MATERIAL

Good hosts and hostesses create environments where people can connect relationally. They know when to help guests connect and when to stay out of the way when those connections are happening organically. As a small-group leader, sometimes you'll simply read a discussion question and invite everyone to respond. The conversation will take care of itself. At other times, you may need to encourage group members to share their ideas. Remember, some of the best insights will come from the people in your group. Go with the flow but be ready to nudge the conversation in the right direction when necessary.

DEPART FROM THE MATERIAL

We've carefully designed this study for your small group. We've written the materials and designed the questions to elicit the kinds of conversations we think will be most helpful to your group members. That doesn't mean you should stick rigidly to the materials. Knowing when to depart from them is more art than science, and no one knows more about your group than you do.

The stories, questions, and exercises are here to provide a framework for exploration. But different groups have different chemistries and different motivations. Sometimes the best way to start a small-group discussion is to ask, "Does anyone have a personal insight you'd like to share from this week's material?" Then sit back and listen.

STAY ON TRACK

This is the flip side to the previous point. There's an art to facilitating an engaging conversation. While you want to leave space for group members to think through the discussion, you also need to keep your objectives in mind. Make sure the discussion is contributing to the bottom line for the week. Don't let it veer off into tangents. Interject politely in order to refocus the group.

PRAY

This is the most important thing you can do as a leader. The best leaders get out of God's way and let him communicate through them. Remember: books don't teach God's Word; neither do sermons or discussion groups. God speaks into the hearts of men and women. Prayer is a vital part of communicating with him. Pray for your group members. Pray for your own leadership. Pray that God is not only present at your group meetings but is directing them.

[## SESSION ONE
THE STORY BEHIND THE STORY]

BIG IDEA

The Christmas story means that even when we face difficult circumstances, we can trust God to keep his promises.

REFLECT

As you prepare to lead each session, we'll provide you with some relevant Bible passages to read and some guidance for reflecting on those passages. This is designed, in part, to give you time to think about the Scriptures you'll be discussing with your group. More important, we hope daily reading will help you connect with your heavenly Father during this Christmas season.

DAY 1

Read Genesis 12:1–9.

During the video for this session, Andy said about this passage: "Abraham believed the unbelievable." How did Abraham's belief influence his actions? Take some time to reflect on how your belief influences what you do and the decisions you make.

DAY 2

Read Luke 1:1–25.

Luke's Gospel doesn't begin with the birth of Jesus. It begins with the birth of Jesus' cousin, John the Baptist. John had a part to play in God's plan. He was to prepare the people for the coming of the Messiah—Jesus. Reflect on the circumstances of Elizabeth's pregnancy. What details stand out to you? Do you think it's important that Elizabeth and Zechariah were old and childless? In what ways does that resonate with the story of Abraham?

DAY 3

Read Luke 1:26–38.

What details stood out to you in this passage? Did you read anything you hadn't noticed or picked up on before? In what ways is the story of Mary's pregnancy similar to the story of Elizabeth's pregnancy? In what ways are they different?

DAY 4

Read Luke 1:46–56.

This passage of poetry is commonly known as the Magnificat. In it, Mary rejoices at being chosen to be the mother of Jesus, praises

God, and recounts his history of being faithful to his people. In what ways has God blessed you? How can you praise him during this Christmas season?

DAY 5
Read Luke 1:57–80.

Reflect on the entire passage, but pay special attention to Zechariah's Song in verses 68–79. In what ways does Israel's long and often difficult history make Jesus' arrival even more meaningful? In what ways do the challenging circumstances in your life make you more appreciative of what God has done for you through Jesus?

PRAY

This week, spend some time praying the following prayer (you don't have to do it verbatim; you can use your own words):

Father in Heaven,

Every year, Christmastime goes by in a blur. Life is busy and stressful, and I find myself focused on things that aren't important in the long run: decorating the house, shopping for gifts, planning menus, arranging travel plans.

Help me slow down a little this year. Help me get the things done that need to get done, while also paying attention to what really matters. Christmas is a time of year when I want to reflect on all you've done for me, praise you, and let you know how grateful I am for your presence in my life.

Thank you for Jesus. It's in his name I pray to you.

Amen.

DISCUSSION QUESTIONS

Use these notes to help you guide the group discussion:

1. How do you feel heading into this Christmas season? Is it a positive or negative time for you?

For many in your group, this will be a light icebreaker question. For some, it may be more challenging. Be prepared for those that have negative Christmas experiences for whatever reason. Remember to thank them for sharing. It will encourage them to continue to be open during future discussions.

2. Do you find it difficult to believe the details of the Christmas story? Why or why not?

After asking this question, spend more time listening than speaking. It's a good way for you to gauge where your group is on this topic. This isn't a time to correct group members or try to convince them the story is true. They'll have four weeks to think about, explore, and discuss this topic.

3. Talk about a time when God seemed silent or distant in your life. What happened? What did that experience do for your faith?

This question may stir memories of difficult times for some. It may even stir some strong emotions directed at God—including anger. Be patient with your group members. Don't try to correct their experiences or explain them away with theology.

If there was a time in your life when you felt abandoned by God, open up about it. Doing so will encourage group members to follow your lead.

4. Read Genesis 12:1–3. In what ways does God's promise to Abraham change your view of the Christmas story?

The best way to navigate this question is to take some time before group to answer it for yourself. Does God's promise to bless all people of the earth through Abraham change the way you think about the Christmas story?

Give your group members space to think before speaking. Try to get comfortable with uncomfortable silences. Resist offering your response first, if possible.

5. Read Isaiah 49:6. What does this verse tell you about God's character? *If you're met with silence when you ask this question, consider this follow-up: "What do you think it means that 'It is too small a thing for you to be my servant to restore the tribes of Jacob and bring back those of Israel I have kept'? What does it say about God that his plans for Jesus were to bless more than just his chosen people?*

6. What can you do this season to focus on the meaning of the Christmas story in our culture and in your life? How can this group help you?

Challenge your group members to be specific when answering this question. What concrete actions will they take? The best way to influence the quality of their answers is to come up with a clear, measurable action step for yourself. What will you do this season to focus on the meaning of the Christmas story?

[SESSION TWO
THE AUTHOR OF LIFE]

BIG IDEA

God gave his one and only Son to demonstrate the incredible depth of his love for us.

REFLECT

As you prepare to lead each session, we'll provide you with some relevant Bible passages to read and some guidance for reflecting on those passages. This is designed, in part, to give you time to think about the Scriptures you'll be discussing with your group. More important, we hope daily reading will help you connect with your heavenly Father during this Christmas season.

DAY 1

Read Matthew 1:1–17.

Matthew begins his story with a long genealogy of Jesus. Why do you think his connection to these people in the Old Testament is so important? How might it change the way you think about the Christmas story?

DAY 2

Read Matthew 1:18–25.

What details stand out to you in this passage? In what ways does Joseph demonstrate extraordinary trust in God?

DAY 3

Read Isaiah 7:13–14.

What does this passage written by the prophet Isaiah indicate about our desperate need for the Christmas story? What are some things that can make it difficult for you to trust God? How does Jesus help you trust despite those difficulties?

DAY 4

Read Acts 3:11–26.

In this sermon to the people in Jerusalem, Peter recounts the history of God and his people, going all the way back to Abraham. Why is this historical context vital to understanding the importance of Jesus? How does it change the way you view your own relationship with God?

DAY 5

Read Romans 5:6–8.

Take a moment to reflect on the words of these verses. What do they mean in your life?

PRAY

This week, spend some time praying the following prayer (you don't have to do it verbatim; you can use your own words):

Father in Heaven,

I recognize that you demonstrated your love for me. Jesus died for me, even when I was resisting you. I'm grateful that you—the author of life—chose to love me even though I didn't deserve it. Thank you for reaching into history and making the Christmas story happen. Thank you for Jesus.

Amen.

DISCUSSION QUESTIONS

Use these notes to help you guide the group discussion:

1. Talk about a time you had trouble convincing someone else of something you knew to be true. What happened?

This question is designed to get your group to think about how difficult it can be to convince someone of something—even if it's true. Listen closely to the stories your group members tell. Later on, you may be able to relate the discussion back to those stories.

2. Read Galatians 4:4–7. In what ways does our culture tempt us to behave like slaves even though we're God's children?

Consider the things we're tempted to choose instead of God. Be ready to share your own example. It will encourage your group members to share theirs.

3. In the video teaching, Andy said, "The events of Christmas would be unbelievable if the story wasn't so remarkable." Do you find the Christmas story unbelievable or remarkable? What are some of the things that have shaped your view of Christmas?

Spend most of your time listening to how your group members respond to this question. Don't correct their theology or try to explain away their doubts. Thank them for sharing. It will encourage them to continue to open up with the group.

4. Read Romans 5:6–8. What are some truths about God that you wouldn't know if Jesus hadn't demonstrated them?

This question is designed to get your group thinking about how essential Jesus is to our understanding of who God is and what he thinks of us. Let your group members speak first. If necessary, allow some uncomfortable silence. Be ready with your own examples if your group seems stuck and you need to get the conversation started.

5. In the video teaching, Andy said, "Jesus' death demonstrated the magnitude of our ingratitude and the magnitude of his love for us." Is it difficult for you to believe God loves you that much? Why or why not?

This may be a difficult question for some group members to answer. If someone is vulnerable, remember to thank them for sharing. Offer encouragement that God really does love us that much.

6. What can you do this Christmas season to show gratitude for God's choice to demonstrate his love for you? How can this group help you?

Be ready to share. Make sure your answer is specific and includes how the group can help you. Your group members will follow your example.

[SESSION THREE
THE MESSAGE OF CHRISTMAS]

BIG IDEA

It is possible to be free from sin, and we can say no to temptation . . . but only because of Jesus.

REFLECT

As you prepare to lead each session, we'll provide you with some relevant Bible passages to read and some guidance for reflecting on those passages. This is designed, in part, to give you time to think about the Scriptures you'll be discussing with your group. More important, we hope daily reading will help you connect with your heavenly Father during this Christmas season.

DAY 1

Reread Matthew 1:1–17.

Have your group discussions given you any new insight into why Matthew would emphasize Jesus' connection to these people in the Old Testament? Have these insights changed the way you think about the Christmas story?

DAY 2

Reread Matthew 1:18–25.

In light of the conversations you've had with your group over the past couple of sessions, do any new details stand out to you in this passage?

DAY 3

Read John 10:1–10.

What do you think it means for Jesus to be the gate for his sheep? What are some ways your life has been fuller because of Jesus' presence?

DAY 4

Read John 10:11–18.

Reflect on some ways Jesus has been your "good shepherd." In the spaces below, jot down three ways he's cared for or protected you.

_____

_____

_____

_____

_____

DAY 5

Read Romans 6:11–14.

What would it be like if you really took to heart the truth that sin is no longer your master?

PRAY

Turn back to the "Reflect" section. Spend some time this week thanking God for the three ways he has cared for or protected you (that you jotted down under Day 4). Tell your heavenly Father what it means to you that he would intervene on your behalf.

DISCUSSION QUESTIONS

Use these notes to help you guide the group discussion:

1. What is one of your favorite Christmas memories? Why is it special to you?

This is a light icebreaker, but don't underestimate what you can learn about the people in your group through simple questions like this.

2. Read John 10:10. Is it difficult to believe that Jesus wants you to have life to the full? Why or why not?

Faith can sometimes feel restrictive because we're asked to control our immediate impulses for our long-term benefit. Verses like John 10:10 can create tension for people. Allow your group members the freedom to express their potential frustrations that following Jesus doesn't always feel like freedom. Listen without judgment. Thank people for sharing.

3. Do you tend to view the story of Christmas as Jesus providing forgiveness for your sins or as Jesus setting you free from sin? What has shaped your view of the Christmas story?

The difference between forgiveness of sin and freedom from sin can seem subtle, but it's important. If we embrace that Jesus has set us free from sin, it will radically change our perspectives and the choices we make. Thinking through your own tensions with forgiveness versus freedom can help you better navigate these tensions. Don't be afraid to share your own struggles. Your group members don't want you to be perfect; they want you to be real.

4. Is it difficult for you to believe that sin doesn't have to be your master and that Jesus has set you free? Why or why not?

Consider the claim that, through Jesus, sin is no longer our master. It's hard to believe, right? Following Jesus doesn't make us instant masters of impulse control. It often feels like sin is still very much our master. Sharing your own struggles can help your group members connect with you and feel free to open up about theirs.

5. Read Romans 6:12–14. What do you think it would look like for you to "offer yourself to God"? How would your daily life be different?

Your group members may struggle to answer this question with specifics. This is especially true of those who need a little time to think and process before they come up with ideas. If you offer specific, concrete examples from your own life, it may help them think of their own examples.

6. Does sin currently master you? What can you do to remind yourself that sin is not your master because Jesus has set you free? How can this group support you?

This is a high-stakes question. You're offering group members the opportunity to open up and be vulnerable with one another. No one may take that opportunity, but be prepared in case someone does. When people choose vulnerability in a group, it's vital that you respond with acceptance and without judgment. Thank the person for sharing. Ask how the group can pray for them or even provide practical help.

[SESSION FOUR
READY OR NOT . . . HE IS COMING]

BIG IDEA

God will fulfill his word despite our weaknesses, doubts, and second-guessing. Why? Because he loves us.

REFLECT

As you move on from this study, we recommend you spend some time reading Luke 1 and 2. That's the advice you gave your group members, and it's great advice for you as well. Consider reading each chapter a few times over the course of a week. When you read a chapter, pause to think about the details that stood out to you (maybe for the first time).

Spend some time praying as well. Focus on thanking God for providing what you really need: a Savior.

PRAY

This week, spend some time praying the following prayer (you don't have to say it verbatim; you can use your own words):

Dear God,

Thank you for the priceless gift of your Son. I'm so grateful that through him, I'm able to have a relationship with you that's free of guilt and shame. Help me slow down during this season and really savor Christmas. Help me remember Jesus and all that he's done on my behalf.

Amen.

DISCUSSION QUESTIONS

1. What are you looking forward to this Christmas season? Why?

This is an icebreaker. Give people time to respond, but don't spend more than a few minutes on this question.

2. Why is it important that people like Abraham and Zechariah were imperfect and sometimes weak in their faith, but God chose to include them in his plan to reconcile people to him?

On the surface, this is a simple question. Try to get your group to wrestle with the tension that a perfect Creator chose to work through imperfect people.

3. Think about the story you heard of Zechariah entering the Holy of Holies with a rope tied around his foot in case the other priests had to drag him out. What does that indicate about how Jesus fundamentally changed our relationship with God?

This question is designed to encourage your group to think about how much more personal our relationship with God is because of Jesus.

Here's a possible follow-up question in case the conversation stalls: "Given the rituals surrounding the Holy of Holies, to what extent do you think Zechariah and the other priests felt their relationship with God was personal?"

4. Do you ever feel like you're not good enough or faithful enough for God to use your gifts and talents in his plans? If so, did this video change your perspective?

This question may be a challenge for some because it requires vulnerability. Listen carefully and actively to how group members answer. Refrain from judgment. Thank them for sharing.

5. What can you do this Christmas to remind yourself that God is going to fulfill his word despite your weaknesses, doubts, and second-guessing?

Ideally, group members will identify specific, concrete things they can do to remind themselves of God's faithfulness. Sharing your own specific example may help group members think of and communicate their own.

6. God loves you so much that he sent his only Son to die in order to set you free from sin. How does that change your perspective on faith? How does it change your perspective on life?

The idea of grace—that God loves us and gave his Son for us, even though we don't deserve it—is difficult to accept in our hearts, even when we understand it in our minds. Give group members space to express doubts. Listen. Thank them for sharing, and share your own experiences. Avoid responding by correcting behavior or offering theological answers.

Are we too familiar with Christmas and Easter?

The stories of Christmas and Easter are so familiar that we rarely dig into the details.

But what if we did?

We might find that they stop sounding like far-fetched fairy tales. In fact, the improbable details of these stories might even start to sound like real life—maybe even your life.

Who Need Christmas
Study Guide
9780310121077

DVD
9780310121121

Why Easter Matters
Study Guide
9780310121091

Available now at your favorite bookstore,
or streaming video on StudyGateway.com.

Once upon a time there existed a version of our faith worth the world found irresistible.

In this book and six-session study, Andy Stanley shows us how Jesus' arrival signaled that the Old Testament was fulfilled and its laws reduced to a single verb—love—to be applied to God, neighbor, and enemy. So, what is required if we want to follow Jesus' example and radically love the people around us? We almost always know the answer. The hard part is actually doing what love requires.

Rather than working harder to make Christianity more interesting, we need to recover what once made faith in Jesus irresistible to the world.

Book	Study Guide	DVD
9780310536970	9780310100492	9780310100515

Available now at your favorite bookstore,
or streaming video on StudyGateway.com.

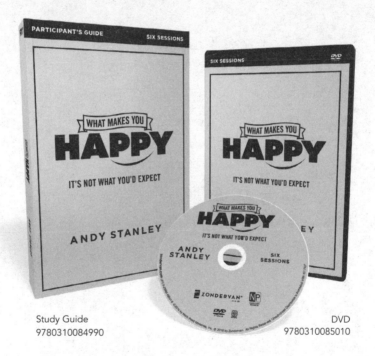

What if you could find a new starting point for faith?

Everything has a starting point—your life, your relationships, your education, your career. Your faith has a starting point as well. But too often, that faith isn't strong enough to withstand the pressures of life. So what if you could find a new starting point for faith?

Welcome to *Starting Point*—an eight-session small group conversation about faith. Whether you're new to faith, curious about God, or coming back to church after some time away, it's a place where your opinions and beliefs are valued, and no question is off limits.

Study Guide
9780310819325

DVD
9780310817734

Available now at your favorite bookstore,
or streaming video on StudyGateway.com.

ZONDERVAN®

Grow an Unshakable Faith

Imagine how different your outlook on life would be if you had absolute confidence that God was with you. Imagine how differently you would respond to difficulties, temptations, and even good things if you knew with certainty that God was in all of it and was planning to leverage it for good. In other words, imagine what it would be like to have perfect faith.

In this six-part series, Andy Stanley builds a biblical case for five things God uses to grow BIG faith.

Study Guide
9780310324232

DVD
9780310324188

Available now at your favorite bookstore,
or streaming video on StudyGateway.com.

 ZONDERVAN®